Beginners to Intermediate

Easy Tunes from Around the World for Clarinet

70 Traditional melodies and rounds from 28 countries arranged especially for beginner clarinet players starting with the very easiest. All in easy keys.

Amanda Oosthuizen

Jemima Oosthuizen

The Catchy Clarinet series
Wild Music Publications
www.WildMusicPublications.com

We hope you enjoy *Easy Tunes from Around the World for Clarinet!*

Take a look at other exciting books in the series
Including: *Christmas Duets, Trick or Treat – A Halloween Suite, More Christmas Duets, Classic Duets for Intermediate players, 50+ Greatest Classics, Easy Traditional Duets, Moonlight and Roses, Champagne and Chocolate,* and many more!

For more information on other amazing books please go to:
http://WildMusicPublications.com

For a **free** sample of our book of **Christmas Carols** (no need to download if you already have the book!) AND a **free play-along backing track** visit:

http://WildMusicPublications.com/553secret-tracks65-clarinet754/

And use the password: **m@DWinds4U**

Happy Music Making!

The Wild Music Publications Team

To keep up –to-date with our new releases, why not **follow us on Twitter**

@WMPublications

© Copyright 2016 Wild Music Publications

The music in this book is protected by copyright and may not be reproduced in any way for sale or private use without the consent of the author.

Contents

A Canoa Virou	16
Ah Ya Zein	33
A My Roschist Chistili	18
Aura Lee	12
Boat on Lake	10
Botany Bay	32
Cader Idris	35
Can Can	27
Clown's Dance	20
Come and Sing Together	24
Dame Tartine	3
David of the White Rock	36
Don't Forget Katie	30
Early One Morning	31
Everybody Loves Saturday Night	29
French Round	3
Giants	8
Greensleeves	37
Go Down Moses	25
Hey Ho Nobody At Home	21
Hine e Hine	10
House of the Rising Sun	32
I Gave My Love a Cherry	22
I Love Sixpence	31
In Spain	15
Izika Zumba	17
Jiana	26
J'ai un Bon Tabac	5
Johnny Todd	21
Kaake Kaake Koodevide	6
Kisnay Baniya	26
Kookaburra	28
La Bergamesca	27
La Folia	25
Lightly Row	4
Lullaby (Basque)	24
Lullaby (Polish)	7
Matilda	34
Miss Lucy Long	38
Morning Has Broken	27
My Bird is Dead	22
My Dame Hath a Lame Tame Crane	11
Nini ya Moumou	5

Old MacDonald	13
Obwisana	13
Phoebe in her Petticoat	9
Pokare Kare	14
Rose Rose	29
Scarborough Fair	23
Seal Woman's Lament	9
Shenandoah	34
Skip to my Lou	8
Sleep Sleep	2
Soley	5
Spanish Ladies	14
The Cuckoo	16
The Dove	12
The Harp that Once Through Tara's Halls	28
This Land is My Land	7
The Londonderry Air	39
This Old Man	20
The Old Tree	2
The Saints	4
The Snow Fell Gently	11
The Three Friends	2
The Three Ravens	30
Tsetang Choung-La	19
Twinkle Twinkle	19
When I First Came to This Land	23
Whisky Johnny	15
Yangtse Boatman	17
Yankee Doodle	6

Information

Tempo Markings
Adagio – slow and stately
Adagio lamentoso – slowly and sadly
Alla Marcia – like a march
Allegretto – moderately fast
Allegretto pomposo – fast and pompous
Allegro – fast and bright
Allegro assai – very fast
Allegro grazioso – fast and gracefully
Allegro maestoso – fast and majestically
Allegro vivace – fast and lively
Andante –at walking speed
Andante maestoso – a majestic walk
Andante moderato – a moderately fast
Andante non troppo – Not too fast
Andantino – slightly faster (or sometimes slower) than Andante
Andantino ingueno – not fast but with innocence
Lento - slowly
Maestoso - majestically
Moderato - moderately
Moderato con moto – moderately with movement
Molto allegro – very fast
Molto maestoso – very majestically
Presto – extremely fast
Tempo di mazurka – In the time of a mazurka - lively
Tempo di valse – In the time of a waltz
Vivace – lively and fast
Vivo - lively

Tempo Changes
rall. – *rallentando* – gradually slowing down
rit. – *ritenuto* – slightly slower

 fermata – pause on this note

Dynamic Markings
dim. – *diminuendo* – gradually softer
cresc. – *crescendo* – gradually louder
cresc. poco a poco al fine – gradually louder towards the end

pp – *pianissiomo* – very softly
p – *piano* – softly
mp – *mezzo piano* – moderately soft
mf – *mezzo forte* – moderately loud
f – *forte* – loud
ff – *fortissimo* – very loud

gradually louder
gradually softer

Repeats
D.C. al Coda – return to the beginning and follow signs to Coda ⊕
D.C. al Fine – return to the beginning and play to *Fine*

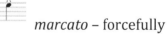 A repeated passage is to be played with a different ending.

Articulation
 staccato – short and detached
sempre staccato – play staccato throughout

 accent – played with attack

tenuto – held– pressured accent

marcato – forcefully

Ornaments

trill – rapid movement to the note above and back or from the note above in Mozart and earlier music.

mordent – three rapid notes – the principal note, the note above and the principal.

 acciaccatura – a very quick note

appoggiatura – divide the main note equally between the two notes.

Sleep, Sleep

Dreamily　　　　　　　　　　　　　　　　　　　　　　　　　　France

The Old Tree

Very slowly　　　　　　　　　　　　　　　　　　　　　　　　Germany

The Three Friends

Lively　　　　　　　　　　　　　　　　　　　　　　　　　　Finland

French Round

Walking   France

Dame Tartine

Carefully   France

J'ai un Bon Tabac

Lively — France

D.C. al Fine
(Go to the beginning and play to Fine.)

Nini Ya Moumou
(Sleep, my Baby)

Rocking — Morocco

Soley

Lively — Haiti

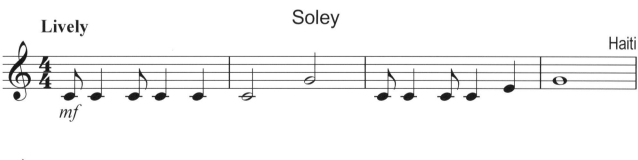

Yankee Doddle

Lively   England

Kakke Kakke Koodevide
(Hey Crow, Where's Your Nest?)

Lively   India

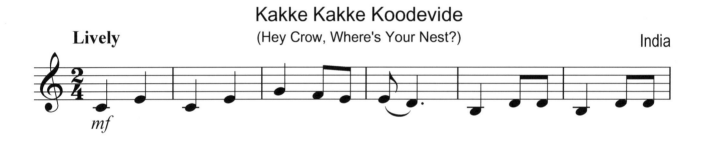

This Land is my Land

Not too fast
USA

Lullaby

Gently
Poland

9

Seal Woman's Lament
(a round)

Sadly   Iceland

Phoebe in her Petticoat

Swishing happily   England

Boat on Lake

Smoothly — China

Hine e Hine
(Little Girl)

Sleepily — New Zealand

The Snow Fell Softly

Gently Lithuania

My Dame Hath a Lame Tame Crane
(a round)

Lively England

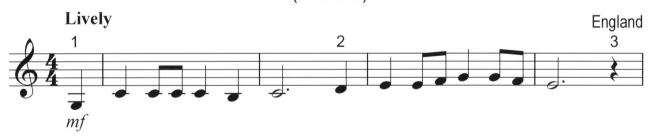

mf

Obwisana
(The rock has hit my hand, Grandma)

Ghana

Old MacDonald

Traditional

Pokarekare ana
(The waves are breaking)

Maori

Eerily

Spanish Ladies

England

Lively

In Spain
(a round)

Not fast — England

Whisky Johnny

Cheerfully — Ireland

The Cuckoo

France

Cheerfully

A Canoa Virou
(The Canoe Turned Over)

Brazil

Running

Yangtse Boatman
(a round)

China

Izika Zumba
(Zulu war chant)

South Africa

Can Can

Lively — Jacques Offenbach

A My Roschist Chistili

Thoughtfully — Russia

Tsetang Choung-La

Smoothly
Tibet

Twinkle Twinkle Little Star

Smoothly
France

This Old Man

Cheerfully England

Clown's Dance

Clumsily France

Hey Ho, Nobody at Home
(a round)

England

Johnny Todd

Scotland

My Bird is Dead
(a round)

Mournfully France

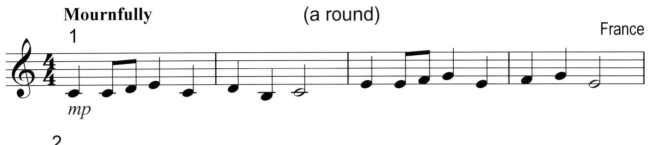

I Gave my Love a Cherry

Not too fast England

Scarborough Fair

Smoothly
England

mp

mf

mp

When I First Came to This Land

Lively
USA

mf

f

mf

Come and Sing Together
(a round)

Hungary

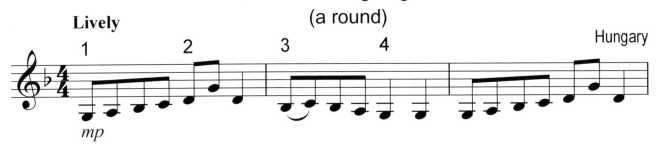
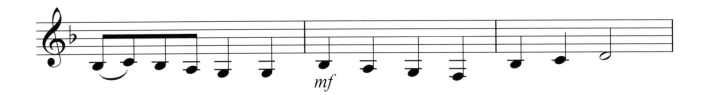

Lullaby

The Basque Country

D.C. al Fine

Go Down Moses

Fairly slowly   USA

La Folia

Steadily   Spain

La Bergamesca

Fast — Italy

Morning has Broken

Gently — Scotland

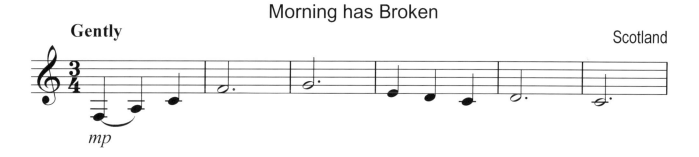

Kookaburra
(a round)

Lively — Australia

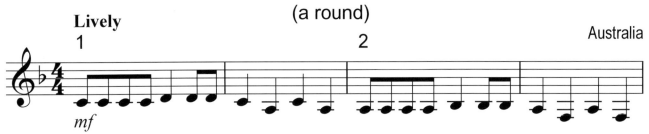

The Harp that Once Through Tara's Halls

Not fast — Ireland

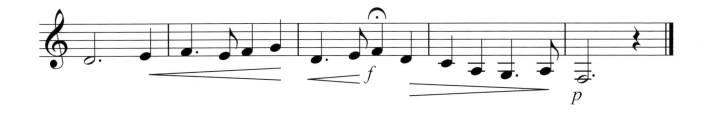

Rose, Rose
(a round)

England

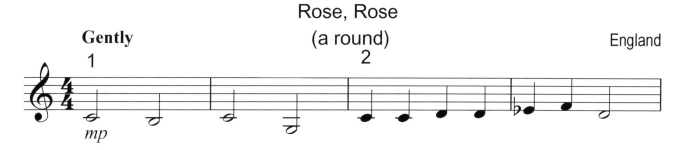

Everybody Loves Saturday Night

Nigeria

Don't Forget Katie

Amanda Oosthuizen

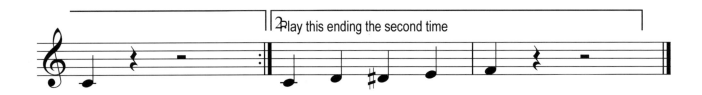

Early One Morning

England

Sweetly

mp ... *mp*

I Love Sixpence

England

Lovingly

mf

House of the Rising Sun

Mysteriously — USA

Botany Bay

Lively — Australia

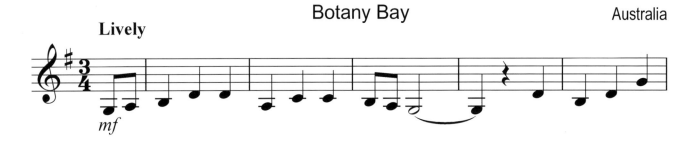

The Three Ravens

England

Ah Ya Zein

Arabia

Matilda

Jamaica

Shenandoah

USA

Cader Idris

Majestically

Wales

David of the White Rock

Wales

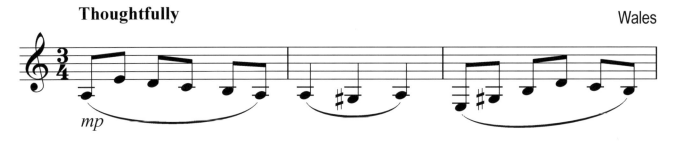

Greensleeves

England

Sadly

Miss Lucy Long

USA

The Londonderry Air

Ireland

Smoothly

If you have enjoyed **Easy Tunes from Around the World for Clarinet,** why not try the other books in the **Catchy Clarinet** series!

For more info, please visit: **WildMusicPublications.com**

All of our books are available to download, or you can order from Amazon.

Introducing some of our favourites:

Champagne and Chocolate

50+ Greatest Classics

Christmas Carols

Trick or Treat – A Halloween Suite

Easy Traditional Duets

Christmas Bonanza

Classic Duets for Intermediate Players

Christmas Duets

Moonlight and Roses

COMING SOON

Made in United States
Orlando, FL
16 January 2023